HIS SECRET OBSESSION

HOW TO MAKE HIM WANT YOU FOR WOMAN
By David Right

PREFACE

Imagine having a fulfilling and committed relationship, but without experiencing anxiety and insecurity, without all of the worry. Imagine enjoying a passionate connection without feeling obsessed with your man, without having to push your relationship in any particular direction by yourself. Picture it! No more sleepless nights, no more fears or uncertainties about where your relationship is going... Can you imagine that?

Most relationships start out with enthusiasm, with endless conversations full of magic moments in which we feel a deep connection, an attraction to this person, as we fall in love. We wonder how it is even possible to feel such a connection with someone we've just met. When we, as women, begin to feel this sort of compatibility, we start to offer everything - our bodies, our hearts - to this man, as if all of our happiness depends upon him.

Here, we see that the more we invest in this relationship, the more he withdraws and the less he participates. There is less communication and less interaction between us. Gradually, he spends a reduced amount of time with us, and slowly, the intensity and intimacy within our relationship begin to fade away. While he doesn't necessarily quit on the relationship, we can feel that something ugly is about to happen.

Obsessively, we start asking ourselves why this happened. What have we done wrong, what can we do to bring him back? How can we change ourselves to better please him? We are overwhelmed with all sorts of fearful and guilty thoughts.

After meeting a man we like, we women just DO, DO, DO whatever we can to show him how special we are. We work like mad for him, doing errands and planning outings, or organizing big surprises for him. We cook, and, more than that, we accept plans and everything else he wants, even if we feel uncomfortable with them - all to make him happy.

Every woman has a masculine and a feminine energy. Every time we want to DO something for a man, we activate this masculine vibe. This is called over-functioning, and it doesn't work in romantic relationships with a man. A man doesn't want to interact with another man that is disguised as the woman he likes. This is the dynamic of relationships, even if it sounds unusual to us as women.

The only way to connect to a man's heart is to function within your feminine energy when you are around your man.

Our feminine energy is reflected in what we are, not in what we do. When you're with a man and living in the moment, enjoying both his presence and his company, you immediately switch to your natural feminine state. He will be relaxed and happy to act in his masculine energy around you.

The BAD NEWS is that when we do these things when we put all of our energy into him and cannot find peace and happiness without him, something dangerous is happening: We forget about ourselves. When a woman is not paying attention to her needs and feelings, she is signalling clinginess, dependence and intense, dramatic, negative vibes. These are the "messages" that men pick up from us which drive them further and further away.

Imagine that you are covered in an invisible balloon of negative energy, and even if you fake a million-dollar smile, men can pick up on this instantly.

The GOOD NEWS is that you can change this vibe if you learn few key secrets that you can apply to your relationship. How do you help the man you love consider himself the luckiest man on earth ? How do you help him share your love and become certain that YOU are the one for him? How do you help him bring out the hero instinct in him? These questions among many others are answered in this book. You will be better off in dealing with your man after reading and following the illusrations portrayed in this book. Read on!!!

Table of Contents

CHAPTER 1- MEN SECRET OBSESSION-WHAT MEN SECRETLY WANT

One key difference I've observed between men and women is that women seem to be much more aware of what they want and need in a relationship...and aren't afraid to express it. Men, for various reasons, aren't always so in tune with what they really need in order to feel loved and fulfilled in a relationship, and the ones who are aware will seldom come right out and say it.

It makes sense from an intellectual standpoint. From a early age women learn to cultivate close, intimate relationships and they learn what makes them feel cared for and understood. Male friendships don't usually have the same depth and level of closeness, so men typically enter the realm of emotional awareness later in life, usually when they form relationships with women.

A guy generally won't ask for what he needs because lot of the time, he doesn't even know what it is. But then when you give it to him, it feels amazing. He feels appreciated and loved, and he comes to love you even more.

And with that, here are the top five things guys secretly love and want from you, but will seldom ask for.

1. Compliments

No man will ever come right out and tell you he likes it when you compliment him because it's a weird thing to ask for, and also not very "manly," if you will. But just because he doesn't ask, doesn't mean he doesn't crave.

Men also feel insecure about their physical appearance, and they don't get nearly as much validation as we do. Think about it, when a guy posts a picture on Facebook or goes out with friends he doesn't have a loyal band of cheerleaders commenting on how great he looks. When it comes to his physical appearance, you're really his only source of compliments, so load him up! Tell him you think that shirt is sexy on him, that you can tell he's been working out hard at the gym, that a certain color makes his eyes look even more striking, that his hair looks sexy pushed back … you get the point!

2. When you ask for his advice

You know how amazing it feels when your man cherishes and adores you and showers you with love? Well he gets the same feeling when you ask for his advice. Men have an overwhelming need to feel useful, to feel like they, have something of value to offer. This is true in all areas of his life and especially so in relationships. He wants to feel like he is adding to your life in a meaningful way, and you can help him feel this way by soliciting his advice and opinions.

When I get relationship ⬜uestions from readers I love sharing them with my husband just to get his take and insights. Usually, I already know the answer to the problem (I've been doing this for ⬜uite a while now!) but I still love sharing it with him and getting his feedback. And he absolutely lights up when given the chance to offer his input.

Men in general are very solution-oriented and thrive when there is something to be solved. That's why a man will typically try to solve your problems when you talk to him about something that's upsetting you, something most women get frustrated by because all we really want in those moments is emotional support, and men don't realize that giving said support is more of a solution to the problem than actually solving the problem! (And if your guy does this, try not to get angry at him, just kindly tell him you appreciate his advice, but right now you just want his emotional support.)

3. When you desire him

You don't always need to wait for him to initiate physical affection. Men love feeling like they're irresistible—like you are turned on by him and can't get enough—so flirt with him, seduce him, initiate physical intimacy. A huge turn-on for a man is seeing how turned on his woman is by him!Guys absolutely love the attention that you splurge on them. Whether you are trying to attract them or have been in a relationship for a long time. Fuss over them and you will be richly rewarded for your effort.

4. When you tell him what you want in a way that makes him feel good

Men want to make the woman they are with happy; this is actually one of the biggest driving forces for a man in a relationship. In fact, if a man doesn't think he can make a particular woman happy, he most likely won't want to continue a relationship with her. And men appreciate it when you tell them how to make you happy as long as it's done in the right way. The right way does not include nagging, guilting, lecturing, or shaming. It entails lovingly telling him what you like and what you want in a way that makes him feel good. Framing something as, "I really love it when you …" rather than "Why don't you ever …" is a good place to start.

When you lecture a man or come down on him for what he's doing wrong, he feels like a failure. He also feels like a little kid being scolded by mommy for misbehaving. When you tell him what you want in a way that makes him feel good, he feels good about doing it and good about himself because he knows how to make you happy.

5. Support

One of the greatest feelings to a man in a relationship is feeling like he has a woman in his corner, someone who believes in him no matter what and sees him for the great man he is and the amazing man he could be. There is comfort in knowing that you will be there for him even if he fails, especially since failure is the hardest thing for men to deal with. When you support him and believe in him, and it comes from a true and genuine place, he feels on top of the world, like he can do anything. Most women don't realize the enormous impact our approval has on men; in fact, I would say your guy is starving for your approval. When you're proud of him, it is a huge driving force. Conversely, when you're disappointed in him, it's crippling and makes him feel like a worthless loser.

All the five things listed actually fall under the umbrella of the number one thing all men want but will never tell you and that is ... appreciation.

Appreciation is probably the biggest motivator for a man and it's something most are starved for. In order to keep your relationship happy and fulfilling, it's crucial to express appreciation for all the things he does, both big and small. As I mentioned, men are starved for your approval and they need to feel like winners. When you express genuine appreciation, you're killing two birds with one stone and giving him the greatest gift you can give. The worst thing you can do is to expect certain things from him or act entitled.

Appreciation isn't just about what he does for you, it's about appreciating who he is. Show appreciation for his good qualities, his values, his ambitions, his life choices. Find those things you love about him and show him you appreciate them. Don't assume he just knows, because he doesn't. This is probably the most powerful and transformative relationship skill that you can ever master.

CHAPTER 2- HOW TO MAKE A MAN GET OBSESSED WITH YOU

Have you ever wanted to make a man want you, but you feel hopeless when it comes to love? Do you keep meeting guys you'd like to know but don't know how to make them chase after you? Are you prepared to do what it takes to find love once and for all? Believe it or not, making a guy want you isn't something that comes naturally to anyone. Every girl has to put some effort into making themselves attractive to guys. These pointers tell you everything you need to know to start making men want you.

Regardless of what, you've seen on TV and in movies, beauty alone can't make a guy want you. Although physical attractiveness is important to getting a guy's interest, it can't sustain a relationship. It is, however, a good place to start.

Have you ever heard that everyone is beautiful in their own way? Despite what popular culture suggests, there is no absolute standard of beauty in the world. In the same way you envy other girls for their hair or their figure, there will always be girls who envy something you have too.

Look at yourself in the mirror and ask yourself what your best feature is, then figure out how to use that to your advantage. If you have great eyes, wear makeup that accentuates your eyes. If you have great legs, start wearing clothes that emphasize your legs. By the same token, if there are aspects of yourself that could use improvement, don't be afraid to address them. A gym membership, for example, can do wonders for your figure.

Beauty, however, is more than skin deep. Beauty alone may be able to catch a man's eye, but attitude and personality are essential for holding his attention. Here too, everyone is different, and thus different tactics are necessary.

If you're a naturally social person, flirting is never a bad tactic for making a good first impression. By showing a guy you're interested in him with body language, you can connect with him on a level that's more in tune with your gregarious nature. If you're more of the intelligent but reserved type, try connecting with men intellectually instead. Don't be afraid of rejection. The key to making a man want you is making a real connection with him. Just be yourself and wait to find a true spark with a man. That spark is a good sign of compatibility, one that will strengthen his interest in you and can ultimately form the basis of a strong relationship.

Apart from that, all the basic rules of personality apply. Negativity turns men off while easy-going and enthusiastic attitudes lead to a good time. Obsessive behavior causes men to be cautious while a pressure-free atmosphere lets guys relax and come out of their shells. The key to making a man want you is really all about being as natural as possible in order to give true love some room in which to take root and grow.

We all have our little tricks on how to be extra seductive and flirty and draw them in if we want to. Most of the time we're not even aware we're doing it, we're just naturally used to turn up the heat and play the game when we're interested.

Still, if you feel like you need to put in extra work and spruce up your style to make him notice you, in fact- scratch that- if you need to learn how to make a guy get obsessed with you like crazy, here's what you should do:

1. Be independent woman

Miss Independent is the one that can make him go out of his mind! There's nothing more enticing than a girl who knows who she is and doesn't need anybody's confirmation or approval. She knows what she wants, how to get it and is never needy or clingy.

This is the type of girl that's going to drive him crazy. She's strong, doesn't rely on anyone and he's hooked. There's just something about the fact that she doesn't need him, but chooses him that's enough to make any man fall madly in love.

2. Leave him wanting more

Always leave him wanting more! Guys like to fight to get what they want. The chase is fun for them, and that's what makes them appreciate it more when they get it. That's just how it is.

So, if he gets all of you on a plate and if you make it perfectly clear that he's the one you want he's going to know he has it easy. And easy isn't going to make him go crazy.

What is going to make him eat from the palm of your hand is you giving him your affection bit by bit. Make him feel like he has to work for it and chase you.

It doesn't matter if he is already your boyfriend or even a husband, you should never forget to make your man want you more.

3.Be unpredictable

Being predictable is boring. It's routine, it's easy. Unpredictable girls, who now how to stir things up are definitely going to catch some attention. When I say 'stir things up' I simply mean step out of the ordinary once in a while. Trust me, he's going to lose his mind if you go and do something that's completely out of the norm.

4. Don't be high maintenance

Most guys find high maintenance girls a bore. I mean, sure they do like a girl who takes care of herself but to be this perfect never-relaxed person all the time is just exhausting, for everyone.

He's going to be pretty drawn in if you show him you're able to make the most of any situation and not worry about the way you look or anything else.

5. Be fun and make him want you more

Everybody loves a fun loving person! And any guy who sees that you're someone who's up for having a good time, doing fun stuff, being active, outdoors, having a laugh is most definitely going to crave your company.

The truth is lots of girls aren't really up for action. They prefer getting pampered, chilling and talking. But a fun loving girl who can get wild and crazy is surely going to make any man go crazy about as soon as he sees her in that light.

6. Confidence is key to making a guy fall in love with you

Here's the best piece of advice anyone ever gave me: people see only what you show them if you present yourself in a certain way that is how they will perceive you. This applies to many things in life, and is absolutely golden when it comes to confidence!

Did you know that most of those people who seem to ooze confidence are actually faking it? The best thing is anyone can do it, and with time, you actually do develop this confident personality you've been portraying for the world to see.

And there's nothing more appealing and captivating than a confident girl who knows her worth.

7. Lock eyes with him and make him obsessed

A good long gaze into his eyes is all it takes to make sparks fly and blow his mind. You two locking eyes at just the right moment can work magic and stir up emotions he didn't even know he has!

8. Surprise him

And I don't mean like throw him a surprise, there'll be plenty of time for that once you get him all for yourself. I mean show him you're so much more than he's been seeing.

If he's used to seeing you all dressed up and acting lady like show him you know how to get your hands dirty and let loose as well. If he's used to you being super responsible and school/work oriented take one day to blow everything off and have some fun, with him.

It is extra hard to keep up with the surprises if you're married. But, you should always have in mind that it is needed in order to be irreplaceable.

Do anything that he would not expect you to do!

The most important thing is that you are still being you, you're just showing him the other side – don't try to be something you're not just to impress a guy! If you do it right he's definitely going to want to see more of what you have to offer!

CHAPTER 3- BRINGING OUT THE HERO INSTINCT IN YOUR MAN

You allow yourself to be saved by him. Look at where you are being overbearing and masculine in your nature. Tone that down. Allow him the ability to be the hero for you.

If that doesn't work, the man might have more feminine energy than masculine energy. Meaning, he likely didn't have a masculine father or male role model in his life. Or, he had a dad that was incredibly hard on him and it shut him down and had him take to being more comfortable being around women. In which case, he learned to be softer.

Sometimes you can shift your self and encourage others to grow and change. Sometimes you can't. If you try and fail many times it's likely you need to accept the man for how he is.

Find little victories for him to overcome for you. Verbal affirmation works wonders for most men - even if it's not their primary love language - it's often close to home in men. Help him to see himself as useful to you - to the family - by setting him up for success and then allowing him to take credit and give him praise for a job well done. This is something all mothers will intuitively, grasp and comprehend. It is very primal, basic, and powerful.

As you honor him and he learns to esteem himself more he will have set backs and you must learn how to re-frame them in his mind. Show him the value of a mistake and teach him not to waste it but to embrace it - and do better next time. Let him decide what ""do better" means as that will carry far more dividends than if you had hijacked his growth.

If you do this consistently and well don't be surprised to find him thriving and being much more confident and loving around you. He will come to see you as a source of strength and encouragement- a sort of emotional safe place. You must respect the power he gives you and not abuse it or him - or he may shun all further efforts from you in the future. You must exorcise great patience and restraint- allowing him to make mistakes and grow while encouraging him in his successes.

I think it could be wise to seek allies in this quest. A professional therapist could do wonders for him. The right one would - the wrong one would be a waste of time and money. If you could evaluate his therapist for him and verify if they would be right for each other it might be better.

Be clear and realistic of your goals and do not burden him with your expectations. Provide a safe place to flourish, as women,are so naturally gifted at doing, and allow him to grow naturally in his own way and time. If he's a cowardly lion and you want Prince Charming for instance - you may be out of luck.

While it's true that men gravitate toward protective roles naturally- if he has given up on himself as a MAN this will be hard. Biology is your ally here if you know how to guide and not drive him - biology can be your friend.

Hormones can have powerful affects upon a mans feelings of manlines. I'd recommend having a full blood panel done by a naturopathic licensed doctor. Again if you meet them first it could be very helpful to know if they are willing to ally with you and to what degree.

Once you have created an environment for healing of the spiritual, emotional and physical - just keep it up. Make sure you have your own support system in place. Once again said therapist might be best as they legally are re□uired to be discreet. Therefore you can get as blunt, angry, or disappointed as you feel the need to with little fear of him discovering such things until you are both ready.

Guys are often very much motivated by their egos. And to be a "hero" is a real ego boost.

So the easiest way to bring out that instinct would be to present him with a job that needs to be done, that having it done would be really cool, and most importantly, that he will be able to do really well, really successfully. Doesn't has to be rescuing a child from a burning building. Could be dealing with a nasty smell in the kitchen, or fixing something that's broken.

Then when he's done it, for you to do a bit of that ego massage that says "oh you are soooooo good at that"

Then he might feel so good he may even go clothes shopping with you. Well, he might.

CHAPTER 4- THE REAL SECRET OF ATTRACTION

The secret of attraction is the unconscious hope for healing and understanding. This is why we are so discriminating in our choice of a marital partner. Not just anyone will do. And when we find the right person we become infatuated and fall head over heels for him or her. Our passion and hope for lifetime mate often borderlines on the absurd. Typically, what we see in him or her is really a self-generated fantasy. We are in "la la" land. We unconsciously block out all of their negative characteristics and distort their positives. We imagine them to be loving, caring, intelligent, funny, patient, giving, attractive, interesting, hard-working when, in fact, they are often very little of all of this. However, and all fairness, in spite of what we think about ourselves, we are also far from this ideal!

The simplest proof that much of what we know about a future mate is "imagined" is demonstrated by the fact that in North America about half of all couples that marry ultimately end up divorced. And of those that remain married, when asked, the majority believe they have chosen the wrong partner. What happens? Why is everybody so disappointed in their mate? Simply, after six months or a year of marriage, when the fantasy bubble pops, then each individual begins seeing his or her partner for whom he or she really is.

One might err in thinking that human beings are totally unsuited for finding appropriate lifetime partners to live together until separated by death. Perhaps we would be more successful if we just roll the dice and let chance determine who our lifetime partner should be. The truth is, however, we are actually very skilled in finding the right partners. Our folly is not knowing what to do when the fantasy bubble pops and problems occur. We often don't know how to properly understand our disappointment and frustration.

To understand ourselves and how during courtship we select a particular person as a mate we must begin by exploring childhood. Childhood is rarely ideal. Most children suffer because of parents who lack appropriate parenting skills or are burdened with their own personal and unresolved problems that negatively impact upon their children. As well, uncontrollable circumstances such as poverty, emigration or illness can negatively affect children. A natural consequence for most children of an imperfect childhood is that some of their basic emotional needs are not completely met. For example, let's consider a boy that is raised by a mother that maintains a position of emotional distance from him as he grows up. As a result, this boy is deprived of the natural emotional support and love that he needs. As a conse□uence, this boy will grow into adulthood with an emotional deficit. In this particular case what is missing is "emotional intimacy." This deficit will then become a strongly felt "core value." When he is married, he will have expectations that his wife will provide for him that which his mother did not. The irony, however ,is that typically the women he will be most attracted to will remind him of his mother, that is, a woman that is emotionally distant or cold.

The reason that he is unconsciously searching for a woman that reminds him of his mother is so that he can reclaim that which he was denied as a child in a form that seems as if he is actually getting it from his mother since his wife reminds him of her. Unconsciously, the debt owed to him by his mother is transferred to his wife. Ironically, he actually picks the most unlikely candidate to give him emotional warmth and closeness since his attracted to somebody that is distant and cold. But she is "like" his mother and he now has a second chance to make-up that which he most missed in childhood. He loves his bride because he hopes and imagines that she will fulfill his emotional needs and thereby he will be healed and become a whole person and then live a happy and content life.

Marital problems usually first begin when there is a realization that a partner is unable or unwilling to give that which is most needed and desired. It is as if the partner is not honouring his or her commitment to meet these deep psychological needs and heal his childhood wounds. The problem in understanding what is really going on is that this complicated psychological process is unconscious for most people and this disappointment is experienced as confusing and undefined feelings. As a result, on a personal level, disappointment, anger and depression often set in. A partner's little daily behaviours can become symbolically irritating and overtime an individual can begin to perceive his or her partner as a "enemy."

However, things can turn out very different if marriage is seen as an opportunity for personal growth. Through emotional and intellectual growth and maturity we can come to understand at some level of consciousness that each person enter into marriage with a hidden agenda. We wants to get from our partner all the positive emotional experiences we didn't get as children. We want to heal our childhood wounds and take away the pain that we still now feel as an adult. In order for this to happen our husband or wife has to become more than he or she already is. For example, a wife who is naturally emotionally distant must change her nature and become warm and communicative to her husband who is in need of emotional closeness. In turn, he too must go beyond himself in order to give his wife what she needs. Marriage provides the opportunity for tremendous emotional and spiritual growth. This great "medicine" can only happen within the marital context. Both individuals in the marriage have the opportunity to grow and heal. When this happens, the result is a happy and satisfying marriage.

We can help actualize this beautiful potential for growth and wholeness by making our unconscious needs conscious, i.e., by identifying our core emotional values and needs. Marital bliss is created when both partners make a concerted effort, as a team, to provide each other with emotional and psychological nurturing and healing.

When a couple is experiencing marital difficulties, rather than making a partner into an "enemy," it should be viewed as an opportunity for personal growth and a clear signal to work hard on establishing marital peace and harmony. With effort overtime, success will come

The real secrets of attracting any man:

Men can be very elusive, it is very hard to know what they want although it is not completely impossible to attract them. Attracting any man can be easy, but attracting a really hot guy can be a real challenge since he's most probably eyed by a million other female species.

There are many tried and consistently rewarding tricks a woman can do to attract the hot guy everyone is raving about. To learn about them, here are some tips.

Let him chase you

Men love the chasing game since they are naturally competitive by nature. Giving him an impression that you are as well eyed upon by other men can certainly make him notice you. A man wants what other men want-it's in their nature to challenge each other in order to win the prize.

Be humorous

Men are attracted to girls who are funny and can make them laugh; this also includes the hot guy you've been eyeing for so long. Make sure to not sound offensive or obnoxious, though, as this will immediately send him running in the opposite direction.

Magnificent grooming

This will make anyone notice you instantly. By dressing decently, you can easily catch the attention of the man you are interested in. Dress sexily without appearing cheap, you don't need to show too much skin. Also, take care that you don't have body odor or bad breath because these are major turn offs!

Give him your full attention

Men want attention because they feel that they deserve it. Any man, in fact, wants a ego booster. They want to know that they are desired and attractive to someone.

Be as confident as you can ever be

Confidence exudes a certain kind of sexuality that these kind of men look for. Since they are hot and attractive, they would want someone who is equally or even more attractive than they are. Nothing makes a woman more attractive than by being confident; with the way she dresses, talks, and moves.

The engaging eye contact

Having eye contact can be an advantage as your eyes speak unspoken thoughts and can easily turn a guy on. Looking him in the eyes for a period of time and then giving off a sly smile will definitely make him look back.

Master the art of conversation

A conversation can make or break a first impression. You need to know more interesting topics to be able to hold a man's attention and you can do this by reading books, magazines and being abreast on current events (and sports!).

CHAPTER 5- IS HE THE ONE?

We get together for many reasons, and not always the right ones.

Inevitably the question comes up... Is he the one? Let's examine essential questions that can help you come to the right answer for yourself. You wants to get this right when, even with the best efforts, it often goes wrong. Let's try to stack the deck in your favor.

Attraction:

Most of us is attracted to novelty because the mind loves it.

Sexual energy is stirred up by the new: new lips, new hips, new eyes, a new embrace. So it is often not hard to get excited about a new romance. It's one reason so many fails. People fall in love with love and not with a person.

The key is to be interested in your partner when the sense of newness fades away and intense interest begins.

Attraction is of the body AND the mind.

Some people are attracted to partners that make them feel safe, while others are excited by that man that they can never truly have. (This is how narcissists thrive!)

As time passes, note whether you remain interested in him. And if it's because he's not emotionally available, get some therapy. Such relationships may get you good intimacy, but he'll inevitably drive you crazy when you sense that you are not as important to him as you may want.

For some, relationships transmute into friendships, where intimacy becomes a bit off-putting if not incestuous. Even if you love him, try not to settle for this. With the addition of children, the partnership may grow but not the lust. Without the glue of attraction, your partner may end up looking elsewhere.

So, you have been with him for some time. Are you still mad crazy about his body? Do you still want him, and want him again? If so, you have something.

Fit:

Personalities can blend together well. They can clash as well. And even if the intimacy is great, not everyone can get along with you... and vice versa. Aristotle taught us the golden mean, and I think it works with relationships as well. Sometimes two extroverts simply re□uire too much energy to thrive. Some of the happiest couples that I've known have a balance between introvert and extrovert.

One carries more color. One keeps things more stable.

Often, it's nice to complement each other. She teaches you to get out more. He teaches you to enjoy the grounding of home. Over the long haul, this kind of balance will play out well. If you are too far apart in the extrovert/introvert dynamic, then problems will arise as you both will fail to get your needs met.

Fit is about balance.Ask yourself if you have a good fit with your potential partner.

Home Life:

After treating countless families and twenty & thirty year olds, it often comes down to what happens during a 24 hour period at home. Do you walk on eggshells? Are you completely comfortable in your own home? Or, do you carry some tension about how he may react to whatever may come up?

Stay with people who co-inhabit an easy home life.

The world is tough enough out there. In fact, it's a pretty cold place.

So your home needs to be a calm, happy respite at the end of the day. If you and your partner are arguing, tense, and never ☐uite settled, please consider seeing a counselor. You are participating in a less than adequate relationship, which has the potential to get worse, particularly with the pressures of money and children. And sometimes people stick in such relationships because that is all they know from their own family of origins or they believe that they can fix a broken person.

Go for a happy and easy home life.

Let the hard stuff happen elsewhere, like at work and such.

Family:

Get to know your partner's parents. How they interact with each other will give you a clue about how your partner will be with you. Do they show love and respect for each other? Or, is it a cold or cranky marriage? And, if they are divorced, get a sense how dignified they were in dealing with the divorce. How people leave partners they used to love says a lot about character. Some divorces work well. And some leave lasting... and open wounds.

While your partner may come from an unhappy background, get a sense whether he has truly dealt with the lack of trust or potential abuse experienced growing up.

These wounds go deep and you don't want to be the displaced object of hurt, anger or control.

There are few more terrible things than to be close to someone who carries a volcano of hurt or anger from the past. You will not be spared.

That being said, many people from wounded backgrounds, whether it's divorce, abuse or even from an intact family with high conflict, can and do develop the determination to do it better with their beloved. Great therapy can truly help. Just make sure that he has done the work.

Money:

The main stressors in marriage, aside from compatibility, are sex and money. You must be able to talk about money openly. What are your expectations...and hers? Do you have a sense of how income will be coming in? Will one of you stay home when children enter the scene?

It is often tough to talk about money because it raises anxiety for all involved and sound trite. If you can't deal with this productively, please consider a pre-marital counselor who can help you get a sense of how you both want to live. You can avoid some nasty disappointments if you talk a bit early on.

Old Relationships:

With regard to old relationships, ask yourself whether he had longstanding relationships or not? You want to be with a person who understands in his gut, what it means to enjoy a long-term relationship year after year.

On the other hand, you don't want to be caught in a rebound situation, which happens more than we might like to think.

You want him to love you for you. Not just because he needs someone now.

The relationship may still work, but the dice is loaded against you because he is entering the relationship to avoid feeling of loss, rather than because he is enthralled with you. Once again, couples counseling may be helpful to tease out what's going on.

If you are marrying with children involved, a ex-spouse may be in the picture. If they are your children, you will have to deal with the complexities of what they should call your partner (not Dad or Mom), and how you will parent together knowing that there is another parent out there who may have a different opinion.

Re-blended families are doable, but not without work.

Handling Conflict:

Finally, look carefully at how the two of you handle conflict. Do you avoid it? Does one of you stuff their feelings? What triggers each of you? Are you or your potential partner so defensive there's never a sorry, or a repair of a wrong?

And how long does it take for the two of you to come back to e⬚uilibrium? Some couples bounce back ⬚uickly. Some hold onto resentment for a long time, only to strike again when provoked.

How you fight and make up is part and parcel of compatibility and making an easy going home. If it's hard to deal with conflict or one of you needs to win at the other's expense, consider getting help - or leaving. It only gets harder when kids, money, illness and outside pressures challenge your marriage.

CHAPTER 6- WHY DO MEN LOOSE INTEREST

The chemistry is strong, you connect, you have fun. You go out again and it's another ace in the hole. Now you start to get really excited...could this be it? Maybe you hang out a few more times, but then something changes. Either you notice that he starts to pull away and seems less engaged (commonly known as "the fade away"), or he just vanishes (a phenomenon known as "ghosting"). You feel completely blindsided and shell-shocked.

What went wrong?

Here is why this situation is so confusing for most women. When a girl loses interest in a guy after a few dates, she can usually pinpoint the reason. Maybe he was too desperate, not intellectually stimulating, too quiet, too loud, too boring, too boisterous—she usually knows exactly what it is that turned her off and can give a reason as to why she doesn't want to continue dating him if asked.

It's not always like this for guys. A guy can go on few amazing dates with a girl and find himself suddenly and inexplicably put off by her. Whereas he was previously texting her throughout the day and feeling a strong desire to see her...he now has no desire to contact her whatsoever. This can be as baffling for guys as it is for girls. When asked, many guys will say they don't know why they were suddenly turned off...they just were.

So why does this happen? Is it really out of the blue without cause or provocation? No, there is a reason. The reason it's so hard to pinpoint and articulate is because it's extremely subtle.

During the first few dates with a new guy, your vibe is typically pretty laid-back and easygoing. You want to explore the possibilities with him and see what he's all about. It starts out light and fun, it's about connecting and enjoying each other's company. After few great dates with a seemingly great guy, most women can't help but get excited about the possibilities. They think of where the relationship might go and they start to invest in a fantasy future.

When this happens, you are no longer in the here and now, seeing the situation for what it is. Instead, your mind is focusing on what it could be and that's when it becomes a problem. You become attached to this fantasy future and then you can't help but stress over it and worries about losing it (even though it's not something you ever really had!). Then your fears and insecurities rise to the surface and seep into your interactions with him.

You begin interacting with the thoughts in your head rather than with the person in front of you. Rather than trying to learn who he is and what he's about, you look at his behavior and the things he says as a means to measure how he feels about you... and whether you're getting closer or further away from your goal of having a relationship with him.

Most guys can intuitively sense when a woman is reacting to them as an object rather than a person, when she is using him as a means to fill a void within herself.

Guys typically don't operate this way in relationships and he can't fully understand what happened to turn this seemingly happy, cool girl into an unpleasant, emotionally-reactive, reassurance-seeking mess.

Why Do We Do This?

All anyone really wants is to feel OK, and most of us don't. When a woman worries and needs constant reassurance, it comes from a feeling of, "I am not OK" and the feeling beneath that is fear. What makes it so destructive is that it's not an overwhelming, gripping fear; it's a vague feeling of unease. It's so quiet and subtle you may not even realize it's there. You know how sometimes you'll go to take a sip of water and you literally can't stop chugging? You didn't even realize you were thirsty, it's only when you begin to quench the silent thirst that you realize how potent it was.

That's kind of what's at play here. It's tough for someone to nail down the source of feeling not OK, but they unconsciously latch onto things that will get rid of this feeling, usually through reassurance or trying to make situations come about that they feel will make them happy and finally grant them relief. This inevitably impacts your vibe, you become a parasite of sorts and everyone you come into contact with is simply a means to an end.

When you meet a guy who makes you feel OK, your need for that feeling becomes overwhelming and you latch on forcefully. You may not even realize you're doing it; it's not something you express outright. But it's there and it comes across, even in the slightest ways. It changes your vibe and your energy and guys feel this.

At this point, instead of him feeling like he's connecting with you, he feels like you're trying to get something out of him. Maybe it's reassurance or validation, or maybe just more of the feeling of being OK.

Guys doesn't know exactly what it is, but suddenly their instincts are telling them to get away. This usually occurs at the point where the woman could no longer keep the act up. Maybe she's trying to appear cool and go-with-the-flow, but in her mind she's already thinking of ways to turn a relationship that's really nothing at this point into something. From that point forward, it's not easygoing and natural, it's her measuring if she is getting closer or further from her goal.

Everyone recognizes when someone has an agenda, it's just something our intuition picks up on and it immediately puts us off. Think about how you feel when someone approaches you and tries to sell something. Your first instinct is typically to get far away from them. It doesn't matter how nice and friendly they are, you can't trust them because you know they want something out of you.

That's the switch guys feel. It's the shift from things being easy and fun to agenda-driven. When the woman feels like she's getting closer to her goal, she's happy and elated. When something happens that makes her feel like she is moving further away, she is gripped by that, "My world is falling apart" feeling and may try to seek reassurance from the guy, either outright or subtly.

You Can't Force Love

When you take a relationship that is brand new and start thinking that it's something, or forcing it to be more than it is, it's game over. Your vibe will become man repelling and before long, he'll be gone and you will be left baffled, analyzing what exactly you did to drive him away. But you won't ever find the answer, because it isn't concrete and measurable.

This is one of the main differences between men and women when it comes to relationships. Men are more in the moment and are able to comfortably enjoy a situation for what it is as it is. Women are always looking for ways to improve the relationship and push it forward. It's not that one gender has it right and the other has it wrong. There needs to be a balance between enjoying the present and comfortably laying the foundation for a future. It just can't be done forcefully.

The best relationships are the ones that unfold organically with two people bringing their best selves to the table and discovering who the other person is and developing an appreciation for that person. It's not about using the other person to gain status or self-esteem or security. A relationship can give you these things, but that's a by-product, not the goal.

Guys Who Lose Interest After The Chase

Guys are programmed to love the chase. They get a rush any time a new woman finds them attractive, funny, smart, and irresistible. They do everything they can just to prove to themselves that they can get the girl.

But once she shows interest and he actually gets her, he doesn't have anything to prove anymore. His fear of commitment kicks in and his first instinct is to run. So he moves onto the next con□uest so he can get that ego boost again by pursuing someone new.

Guys who need the ego boost of a new conquest are insecure. They lose interest when a girl shows interest because on some level they feel unworthy. They need to go chase after another girl to feel worthy again.

I know a guy who once told me that any time a girl he liked started to like him back, he'd think there had to be something wrong with her if she liked him. His insecurity about himself made him lose interest in any girl who actually liked him because he didn't feel worthy of her liking him in the first place.

Guys who fit into this category are emotionally unavailable and were never interested in being in a relationship in the first place. So how can you avoid these kinds of guys and attract more secure men with substance who are actually looking for relationships?

Don't fall for it when a guy feeds you a bunch of lines and comes on really strong on the first few dates. Confident guys with substance don't need to do this. Instead, look for the guy who's more discerning. A guy who's really serious about being in a relationship won't show his feelings until after he's gotten to know you and decided you are the one for him.

CHAPTER 7- LEARNING TO UNDERSTAND YOUR MAN

If you've often thought that you and your partner seem to be speaking completely different languages, then you might be right.

Now British relationship coach Julie-Anne Shapiro has used the word 'Menglish' to illustrate how differently the sexes think and hear things.

She claims that men and women do have their own unique languages which sometimes make it feel as if they are on different planets.

But rather than just continuing feeling as if you are banging your head against a brick wall, these are steps which will help you perfect your 'Menglish'.

'If you can learn to respond and communicate in a certain way then it's going to be beneficial for everyone. 'Women find that they are more likely to get what they want if they know how to communicate with their guy and men also find it useful to know that women to talk in a different way from them.

'It's just about raising awareness all round so each side can have a bit more patience and understanding towards their partners.'

1. Don't expect your man to multitask.

Don't talk to him about important things or your relationship when he is doing something else. The likelihood is he won't pay attention and you will take it personally and get upset. It's not that he's not interested, but just that he works best by focusing on one thing at a time and giving it his full attention.

Solution: Be patient. Wait until he's finished what he is doing and then talk to him so his full attention will be on you.

2. Remember the 30 second rule.

If you ask a man for his opinion or how he feels he is likely to take his time to answer. Women are mostly run by their feelings and can usually express them easily but a man holds a whole well of information and feelings but he doesn't express it in the same way.

Solution: Ask him a question then wait 30 seconds for him to answer. During this 30 seconds say nothing. Don't make suggestions, don't try to hurry him along and definitely don't interrupt or talk over him.

You will usually find that by the end of the 30 seconds he will start to talk – this is the time to listen with no interrupting.

Once he trusts that you are not going to interrupt him, talk over him or tell him what to say, he will express more and more to you, including how he feels.Lack of communication can mean a minor disagreement can turn into a major argument

3. Men are problem solvers.

It can be frustrating when you tell your man about your bad day and he starts telling you how to fix it and what you can do about It when all you want is for him to listen to you.

While a woman finds huge relief in talking and talking, men are problem solvers – that's what they do. They see you are upset and they want to solve it to make you happy.

Solution: Before you launch into how bad your day was, explain to your man that you would like him simply to listen while you vent. If you would like him to say anything or help you solve anything, let him know. You'll find he gives his full attention to listening and you feel loved, heard and relieved.

4. Men have limited capacity for detail.

Women sees details. Men on the other hand focus on the facts and get to the point. So when you start telling him all of the details of your day, you can only keep his attention for so long. He is listening for the main point and if it's too long before you get to it, a man will find it almost torturous which is when he starts to withdraw from the conversation.

Solution: Get to the point! Save all the details for your girlfriends. Realize that your man isn't being rude, he is simply being a man. He is interested in what you are saying and wants to hear it but he simply needs less detail so that he can fully engage.

5. Don't expect your man to magically know what you need.

Your man is not a mind reader. It is not his responsibility to automatically know what you need but it is your responsibility to ask. If you don't ask, the chances are your man won't know and won't give it to you, or he may try to guess what you need and get it wrong which then makes you upset and frustrated.

Solution: First, be sure to know what you need yourself. The more specific you can be the better. Men are very logical and respond best to clear, specific information so avoid being vague.

So for example, let's say you would like more affection. Rather than saying 'I would like more affection' you might say: 'Please would you give me a hug every morning before you go to work.'

6. Men thrives on appreciation.

When a man does things for you and you don't appreciate him, you criticize his efforts or you complain, a man feels disheartened. You then wonder why he doesn't enthusiastically want to continue trying to please you and you feel hurt.

Solution: Appreciate what he does for you even if it's not quite what you want. If you need something else be clear and specific. The more you appreciate your man, the more he'll want to give to you.

7. Men are providers

Men are natural providers and need to know what they provide for you. Let's say your man gives you something and you seem to like it but don't tell him why he may well forget to provide it again.

Solution: As part of telling him how much you appreciate him, tell your man specifically what he provided or will provide for you. For example: 'When you hug me and stroke my hair, I feel totally safe and loved.'

8. Men need you to be receptive.

When your man tries to give you something, whether it's a compliment or he wants to do something for you and you won't let him, he feels sad and even crushed. You may wonder why you don't seem to get what you need, perhaps not realizing that you are pushing him away.

Solution: Allow him to carry your suitcase, open a door for you or run your bath. You can make some suggestions of the things you would like, but allow him to choose from your suggestions.

Let him surprise you and be receptive to his ideas too. He'll simply love surprising you and making you smile.

9. Men want to make you happy.

Men are all about winning and your man needs to know that he can win at making you happy. If he sees you sad, complaining, criticizing him and constantly unhappy, eventually he will give up and think that another man can do a better job. You are left wondering where it all went wrong.

Solution: Start to trust that your man really does want to make you happy. Your trust will make him be a better man for you. Focus on and tell him the things you appreciate about him and what he provides for you. Ask for what you need in clear, simple and specific terms. And smile!

10. Confidence, the number one quality a man looks for in his ideal woman

Your man feels genuinely sad when he sees you beating yourself up or saying how fat your stomach is, how frizzy or flat your hair is, or how you wish you were slimmer, fitter, younger or more attractive. He sees you as beautiful, lovable woman – that's why he's with you.

Solution: Be confident in who you are. If there are things you would like to change, do so because you love yourself so much that you're worth it.

When you know your worth you are incredibly attractive to your man and he'll find you totally irresistible.

CHAPTER 8- HOW TO KEEP YOUR MAN INTERESTED IN YOU

Okay, so once you learn how to attract the right kind of guy, how do you keep him interested?

Even a guy who's emotionally available and secure with himself can lose interest if you move too fast for him. It's important to take things slowly.

Don't give him everything all at once.

Don't start texting and calling him all the time and clearing your schedule for him. Don't bend over backwards to get him to like you and make things work out.

If a guy feels like you are more invested in the relationship than he is, your perceived value goes down and he loses interest. When he has to work for you, your perceived value goes up.

Only make him a priority in your life when he's earned it. At every step in the relationship, guys want to feel like they're earning the investment you give them. If they've done nothing to to earn it and you're overly invested, he'll lose interest.

So if you're wondering what you should do to keep him interested, the answer is actually don't do anything. If you have to do something, it means you are trying to push him into something.

Guys don't want to be pushed into anything. They want to come to a decision about a woman on their own. If they feel like they were forced into something too soon, they'll start to pull away.

So if he hasn't called you back, ignore the instinct to call him so he doesn't lose interest in you. This will only make you seem needy and desperate. When a guy is really interested in you, he will call you.

The best thing you can do is stay busy. Go out and have fun without him. Hang out with friends, have some me time, and enjoy life. If you stay busy, he'll be too worried about whether you're available to lose interest.

But I just want to be clear about one thing here. When I say stay busy, I'm not talking about playing games and making him think you're busy when you're really just sitting at home waiting by the phone for him.

Don't put your energy into convincing him you have a life, put your energy into actually having a life!

Don't Jump The Gun

It's also important to be in the present moment. If you think too far ahead into the future and get too serious too soon, it can scare him off.

When you start building a relationship up in your head into something it could be in the future, rather than what it is right now, you're jumping the gun. Have fun and enjoy the moment.

Guys take things one step at a time, while women are more likely to think into the future. When you're just starting to date a guy, you're not going to know right away if he's the one, so just relax and try to have fun in the here and now.

If you start sharing your feelings or making future plans before he's thought about that stuff, he will feel that you are more invested in the relationship than he is. Relationships don't work when one person jumps too far ahead of the other person.

When you jump ahead of him and push the relationship into the future to soon, he's going to feel like you're forcing it on him. He won't feel like it was his choice.

How To Build Attraction

You want to build up enough attraction in the early stages of the relationship so he feels strongly enough about you to commit to you on his own accord. When it's his choice to commit to you, then you've really got him.

So how do you build the attraction? Guys fall in love based on how they feel around a woman. If you're constantly texting him to find out where he is or pressuring him by asking him where the relationship is going, he's not going to feel good around you.

Be confident, playful, and self-assured. Have fun. Laugh. Go with the flow. Make him feel good around you in the present moment so that he wants to spend his future with you.

Be the best version of yourself. The version of you where you're just doing your thing, chilling with friends, and having fun. Don't be the crazy, insecure version of yourself who's constantly wondering if you're good enough for him.

Don't let your emotions get the best of you. If you're feeling insecure because he hasn't called, go out and have fun with your friends. Don't let him know you're insecure about it. Make him work for you.

If he loses interest and pulls away, let him. Keep it drama free. Recognize that you can't force him to be interested in you. If he's the right guy for you, he'll realize what he's missing out on and he'll feel safe enough to come back because he knows you aren't pushing him into anything.

CHAPTER 9- OBSESSION LOVE PHRASES THAT CAN MAKE ANY MAN FALLS FALL YOU

Have you ever seen a woman who can make any guy go absolutely crazy for her, and do the dumbest and sometimes even the most embarrassing things to please her?

And at the same time have you ever seen a woman who does everything right, yet she is never able to get the love or attention she desperately desires from her man?

Most women don't get this; in fact, most women dress sexy, cook great meals and try to logically convince a man to like them. But that doesn't work because they're missing the most important element of the puzzle.

That element is "EMOTION".

If you ever want a man to have deep intense feelings for you, then you need to become emotionally in-tune with him. What do I mean when I say emotionally in-tune? I basically mean that you have to connect with the emotional part of his mind rather than the logical part. But how does one do that?

Here are 6 emotionally stimulating phrases that will absolutely blow his mind and steal his heart in just one conversation. And yes, he'll thank you for this...

1. "I'm proud of you."

Whether he is an amazing dad, works hard at his job, or he's just an all around amazing guy, tell him how proud he makes you. Men don't always get the credit they deserve. Did he get that promotion at work that he's been working towards all year, or does he take care of his elderly parents without fail every day? Tell him how awesome he is; make this weekend all about him and show him what a great job he is doing with a night out or a surprise favorite meal and dessert!

When you show him how proud of him you really are, it not only makes him feel supported, desirable, and secure, it also makes him feel that you "get" him. This is paramount in creating a connection between the two of you as every man deeply craves to feel understood.

Try the Whiz Bang Phrase and the Emotional Transparency Phrase (a subconscious bonding phrase) to show that you're the woman who actually "gets" what he needs.

2. "I want you now!"

This single sexy phrase makes him drop everything (pants included) and start drooling over you.

Whispering almost any naughty line to a guy is the sexual equivalent of 3-D glasses – it heightens the entire experience for him. But after talking to a bunch of men recently, I learned there are four specific words every man longs to hear the most. The phrase that unleashes his lust? "I want you now." Why do these words yield so much seductive power? Relationship expert Felicity Keith explains it in her article, "4 Reasons Why Naughty Talk Drives Men Crazy With Desire"

Men love suggestive comments; just like a woman feels more confident when her man tells her she's beautiful, men feel more confident when their mate finds them sexy and strong. Notice your man's muscles and flirt with him. Tell him he's handsome. Let him know that he's sexy. Your being suggestive makes him feel like he's doing a good job being your man.

Try the "Secret Fantasy Phrase" to become the object of his deepest fantasies and watch how thinking about you turns him on in ways which can't be described by words or the "Razzle Dazzle Phrase" to make every nerve in his body stir and tingle with attraction.

3. "I love you."

Sometimes when we're so comfortable in our relationships we don't say "I love you", as much as we should. These three words have so much meaning behind them, but we tend to just go about our day without saying them. So the next time you're at work thinking of your guy, just send him a little text to show him how much you love him.

4. "You make me SO happy."

We generally accept that men like to be successful in business. They also like to succeed with the ladies, so be smart and let your man succeed with you. Men are more driven to please women than most women realize.It was to win back Helen of Troy that King Menalaus sent the entire Greek army after her, which started the Trojan War, and eventually brought down an empire.

Letting your man know he is succeeding with you won't spoil him or motivate him less; it will motivate him more. It feels good to feel like a winner. Let your man win with you and watch him start looking for ways to please you over and over again.

5. "You look great."

Men have insecurities, just like women. And whether he shows it or not, sometimes he's wondering if his shirt looks better tucked in or out, or if his belly is sticking out a little too far over his belt. This is an especially good compliment if he's been going to the gym—why do you think he's doing all that working out?

A simple phrase like "I love your [insert body part]" will do the trick! Sometimes it helps to get specific. "I love your you-know-what" (or whatever word you can say without laughing or blushing too much.) will drive him wild. Men are sensitive about their manly bits and they want to know that you're attracted to what they have.

6. "I love how strong you are."

Since you're already telling him how much you love how he looks, go a little further and say how strong he is as well. All guys built or not, like to hear that they're strong and can do something special for their partner.

Even more importantly, show him how mentally strong you think he is. Men are no different than us, they like to feel wanted, needed, and that you can lean on them for emotional support, too.

So, do you now realize just how important words are in intensifying feelings of attraction and desire in your partner? Saying the right words can literally make a man's eyes intensify with desire and make his body buzz.

There are certain phrases that have been researched for years and work because they sink deep into the emotion producing part of the human brain and spark up any emotion you want a person to feel. These phrases create a feeling of euphoria in the human brain exactly like a drug and release something called the pleasure bonding chemical throughout his body.

6 Ways to win his love

What makes a man love only you? Here are six great secrets that will lead to the love of your life.

Secret 1: Show him your best. This means that when he sees you, you look great and are in a happy, friendly mood. You take good care of yourself and are fun to be around. This will keep him coming back.

Secret 2. He does the chasing. Don't ignore him but let all suggestions of dating come directly from him. That way he knows you are challenging and confident.

Secret 3. Laugh and relax. Let the relationship take a natural course. Don't be too intense, don't make him feel pressured or let yourself become too obsessed.

Secret 4: He takes the lead. Once you are dating, let him decide where the relationship will go and how fast. This doesn't mean you let him rush you into sex. Sex should be completely in your control, and it is best to wait. He takes the lead means you let him decide when you go from dating to boyfriend and girlfriend, and beyond.

Secret 5. Make him comfortable. Let him know he can be who he is. When he is with you, he should not feel like you expect him to be anything but who he is. He should always look forward to seeing you and having a good time.

Secret 6. The last and most important of six sure ways to win his love: Be patient. Guys comes around in their own time. If he has given you his attention and stuck by you thus far, chances are, he really likes you. When he is ready, he will let you know he loves you. Let him say it first, and immediately let him know you love him too.

Love is a wonderful and challenging thing. Follow these six sure ways to win his love and you will see, in time, that love will come to you. Be sure to love yourself, also. Being confident and happy with yourself will make you a better partner and will help everyone see what a prize you are.

CHAPTER 10- CONCLUSION

Don't just look for the right one; be the right one.

Finding the right man is important. Finding the perfect man, however, is completely unrealistic. What's more, guys can often tell you're subconsciously expecting a Superman that they can never live up to, so they back away.

Instead, find a great man by being a great woman. Don't just look for the right traits in him, but work on the right traits in you. And that starts with your own relationship with God.

"You can't force a woman into a right standing with God, no matter how cute she might be," Mike, a single guy in his mid-20s, told me recently. He added, "I think truly godly women don't try to get attention for being that way. There is a certain feeling a man gets when he is being drawn in by a truly godly woman. She can't fake it."

So work on yourself. Face the fact that you tend to snap at people under pressure, or stretch the truth when cornered; that will pay off in a more appealing character and confidence anyway.

Be confident in yourself, not desperate.

Ask your close friends — the ones who will be honest — whether you come across as confident or as desperate around guys. The first is attractive; the second a turn-off. You may find you've been signaling desperation by something as simple as always putting your hand on a guy's arm or always trying to sit next to him when the gang goes for pizza.

Most of all, don't look to a guy to make you feel complete. Only God can do that; only He can handle that pressure. Instead, relax and be confident in who you are and who He has made you to be. As Mike mentioned earlier: That's attractive.

Take care of yourself.

When promised total anonymity, the men in my research for For Women Only were honest about something awkward to discuss but important to know. The brain wiring governing attraction simply functions differently for a man than a woman; most men have to be visually, physically attracted before they can see a woman as anything other than a friend. Which means it is vital for him to see that a woman takes care of herself physically.

That doesn't mean she has to be a supermodel. In fact, the guys emphasized they loved our individuality and wished we weren't so paranoid about it. But it does means that the physical "spark" more likely comes when a woman takes care of herself and stays healthy (which is also another signal of that confidence we talked about earlier).

Quietly let him know you're interested in him.

So now let's move to the next level. Suppose you are in fact in a good place physically, spiritually and emotionally, and a certain someone has caught your eye. What do you do now? Well, the best thing you can do is get to know him as a friend but in a way that lets him know you prefer his company over others. That way he won't feel it is such a risk to try to move beyond friendship.

Many men told me that when it comes to women, "guys are chicken." They won't risk humiliation if there's a chance they'll be rejected, so they need to have a pretty good idea that you're interested before they'll take that step.

"For me, body language goes a long way," Mike said. Then he laughed, "And I don't mean sexual body language. That means she needs to be drawn closer to Christ, which means I need to switch to personal ministry instead of personal chemistry! But if I can see a confident, yet relaxed expression on a woman's face, coupled with signals that indicate she is being more than 'just friends', I can certainly take a hint! And for a more direct approach, I would personally prefer an invitation to a group gathering or low-pressure date like coffee."

I asked another single man, Dave, what the more-than-just-friends "signals" were. "She can spark my interest by not being pushy, encouraging me, and doing things that I enjoy."

Now you may think Dave's advice sounds pretty generic, but as you'll see shortly, some vital wisdom is buried in those words — both to begin a relationship and as you deepen it.

Let him lead.

As you saw from Mike, it's not that guys always dislike a girl making the first move. But if a girl does that consistently, it allows a guy to be passive. Actually, it encourages him to be passive. Guys are stirred to action by both sensing a woman's interest and by feeling the need to be the leader in the relationship.

That means not pursuing him, letting him make most of the first moves to ask you out or turn a friendship into a romance, and — perhaps hardest of all for us gals — stopping yourself from rushing or forcing your relationship over time.

My husband, Jeff, and I met during what was my first year of graduate school and his last. We got to be good friends over the course of six months, did a lot of things together in groups, went to lunch after church with just each other, and spent a lot of time hanging out — all with absolutely no signals from him as to whether he was thinking about anything more. It drove me nuts. I wanted to make something happen, especially since he was about to graduate! Didn't he realize that if he graduated without any kind of definition to our relationship that the distance would sink us?

Well, this was my first lesson in learning how to respect and trust a man: by not trying to control everything, which, since respect is a man's greatest emotional need, is what a man most needs to see in a woman for a long-term relationship.

What I didn't know was that Jeff was pondering the exact same things and praying about it. For months, he had been talking to his pastor and friends in-depth behind the scenes. It was torture for me, but thank God I didn't try to take matters into my own hands. Like most guys, Jeff needed a woman who would be willing to trust him both initially and for all the years to come.

With that said, pray for discernment and guidance. If he doesn't seem to be interested in deepening your relationship (even your friendship), there's always the possibility that you're holding onto a hope that isn't going anywhere. If so, you would do far better to open yourself up emotionally to others. It may help to seek counsel from wise friends (who know both of you), and be willing to listen if they break it to you that he just doesn't seem interested "that way."

Men love hearing that you admire them. Finally, as you deepen your friendship and eventually your romance, the guys were very clear about what most appealed to them: They love knowing that their woman admires them.

Another thing my research taught me is that no matter how confident a guy looks on the outside, on the inside he is always afraid that he's going to be found out as an imposter. Every day he worries that someday, someone is going to realize he has no idea what he's doing at work, as a boyfriend, in his activities, and so on, and everything is going to fall apart. The secret cry of a man's heart is, "Do I measure up? Does anyone thinks I'm good at what I do?" And he is looking to those around him for the answer to that question.

And that most especially includes you, his girlfriend. You have a unique ability to speak life into a special man. And in doing so, you will touch his heart in a very deep way.

Tell him you're proud of him for being so good at something he does well — whether it's his job, the way he handled that difficult situation at church, or even beating the last level of his favorite video game. If you think he's godly, romantic and funny, let him know. Don't leave him guessing at how you feel about him. And believe it or not, the most important words that will win a man's heart are not "I love you," but "thank you." Thank him for what he does for you ("thanks for coming over and fixing the sink for my roommate and me; you're awesome") and that will win his heart more than almost anything else.

I know it may sound like you're just puffing up his ego, but this isn't about ego. For a guy, it's about knowing that a special woman believes he can take on the world. A world he ultimately wants to share with a special woman, just as much as you want to share it with a special man.

Tips on how to win your man back

Let's be honest --- winning back your man will be alot harder than winning over a new man. But if you want to keep fighting for him, then he must be worth it. If you want to win your man back, you have to reflect on what went wrong, work on improving yourself, and then make a move at the right time. If you want to know how to win your man back and avoid further heartbreak, just follow these steps.

Give yourself some space. If you're constantly around your former flame, you won't be able to step back and actually get some perspective on what went wrong. Though you don't have to ignore him, you should not call him, go out of your way to talk to him, or even Facebook him right after your relationship ends. It's time to be alone for a while, even if that means not going to a party if you'll know he'll be there at first.

Once you're away from the guy, you'll have a less biased perspective about how you really feel and what you loved so much about the relationship.

If you're away from him, he'll start thinking about where you are. You'll already make him want you more just by pulling away.

Think about what went wrong. Before you can try to make things right, you need to be honest about what went wrong in the relationship. Take some time to do some soul-searching and ask yourself what ended the relationship. Where you too moody, too distant, or too flirtatious with others? Think about what you can do to change the dynamic.

You should only try to win him back if you think you can make things different next time. If you ultimately broke up because you were incompatible and just could not make things work, then it'll be harder to win your man back than if it was just because you didn't make enough time for him.

Make a list of all the things that went wrong, and highlight the things you can control.

Ask if you were just going through a difficult time in your life or dealing with a major change. You may be more ready for a relationship if you feel more stable and positive.

Change your ways

Once you've figured out what you may have done wrong in the relationship, resist the urge to call the ex and show off your new found self-realization. Actions speaks louder than words. Just be the new improved self, and word will spread.

If the relationship ended because you were too clingy, work on not being so attached to him. Play it cool and he'll see that you're a new person.

If the relationship ended because you didn't give him enough attention, start making him feel special. Tell him he looks nice and that you're happy to see him.

If the relationship ended because you spent too much time flirting with other guys, don't let him see you with other guys too much or he'll be reminded of why things didn't work out.

Improve Yourself

Look and feel your best. Get your nails and hair done. Take a nice warm bubble bath, and pick out a nice outfit. Once you look your best, you will begin to feel your best. You don't need to get a complete makeover if you want to change. You just need to pay extra attention to grooming and hygiene and the rest will follow.

Spend an extra 10-15 minutes getting ready in the morning and you'll start to feel better. Maybe you were too busy or stressed out to care about your appearance before.

Get a fun hair cut. Nothing makes you feel like getting a fresh start like a fresh cut.

Stop caring about what other people think. If you're so insecure that you spend all of your time thinking about how others perceive you, then you'll never be able to work on yourself enough to catch your former man's eye again. It doesn't matter if people think you're funny, cute, or charming -- it's all about thinking positive things about yourself.

If you don't care what other people think about you, then you'll exude confidence and your former guy will be impressed that you finally know how to do your own thing.

Don't worry about his friends. Maybe his friends didn't think you were right for your former man or just didn't get along with you. You should be nice and get in their good graces, but don't bend over backwards trying to charm them or you'll lose sight of your target.

Stay busy doing the things you love. If you're busy with schoolwork, friends, and pursuing your interests, you will be able to grow as a person and to continue improving yourself instead of pining after your guy. Plus, if he sees that you're obviously occupied instead of sitting around staring up at the sky, then he'll see that you have a lot to contribute and that you're person with an active and engaging life.

Let your former guy see you doing the things you love, whether it's immersing yourself in your studies or going out for a nice run.

Spend lots of time with your friends. They'll be able to keep you positive and will lend you a fresh perspective.

Don't use a rebound relationship as a means of staying busy. This will only distract and confuse you even more.

Develop and express your individuality. As you continue to pursue your interests and get some space away from the guy, you'll start getting a better sense of yourself as an individual, not just a hurt ex-girlfriend. Take this time to really be your true self and to let the world know who you are.

Dress to impress. Wear clothes that really make you stand out as an individual. You don't have to wear anything garish to get attention -- just be brave and wear a "fun" outfit you were too timid to wear before.

Express your individuality by being creative. Write a story, pick up an acting class, or sign a song at an open mic. Let your former man see you being comfortable with expressing your individuality.

Make Him Want You Again

Develop confidence. Assertiveness and self-confidence are naturally attractive to most people. Showing your guy you're capable of being happy is appealing and brings a natural desire. If he sees that you're happy with who you are and what you do, he'll want you even more. Here's how to develop confidence:

Become a more positive thinker.If you learn to see the good in the world instead of the bad, you'll give off an irresistible positive energy, and your guy will want to be around you again.

Be happy with your appearance. Think of at least three things you love about yourself, and dress to show off your best assets. Make sure to get regular exercise to stay mentally and physically strong.

Be assertive. Speak in a clear and effective manner instead of mumbling or talking softly. Command attention with your voice, and everyone will see that you're confident about what you have to say.

Be more classy. It's fun to be in a party and dance alot, but that's not always classy behavior. If you're at a party, the classy behavior is to socialize, but speak calmly, not monopolizing all the attention. You can still get a little crazy as long as you don't get sloppy and he'll like you even more for it. No one wants a girl who is falling down drunk or fighting for all of the attention in the room.

Being classy is a form of being mature. Every guy wants a girl who is mature and in control of her emotions instead of a hot mess in public.

Dress elegantly. You have to look classy as well as be classy. You can show some cleavage but don't wear anything so scandalous or tight that it looks like you're desperate or just trashy. If you look cute but classy, your former flame will naturally notice you.

Let him see you having a great time. Have a big smile on your face and let him see you really enjoying yourself and bringing pleasure to the world and the people around you. You should not have to fake it. If you really want him to want you, then you should actually be having a great time, and be comfortable enough to be happy without him.

Laugh -- alot. Let him see you laughing and giggling with friends and really having the time of your life.

Be engaged. Be fully engaged in whatever conversation you're having. Let him see you being animated, gesturing, and making great points.

Let him see you engaging in fun activities. If he sees you laughing it up at trivia night, having a great time running with a girlfriend, or hitting up the dance floor, he'll want to spend more time with you.

Avoid desperate behavior like the plague. If you're desperate to get his attention, make him see how much fun you're having, or to look so hot that he falls over, then he'll be able to tell right away. Just work on being your best self and hope he catches you in the process. Don't overdo it, or you'll only make things worse.

Don't try too hard to look like you're having fun when you're around him. Let it be natural.

Don't try too hard to look good around him, either. Dress appropriately for the occasion and don't wear much more makeup than usual or incredibly high heels just to catch his eye. He will notice you this way -- but not in a good way.

Don't cling to him. Let him come to you. If you're at a party, let him come up to say hi first.

Make a Move

Tell him how you feel. Once you've reflected on what went wrong, improved yourself, and caught his attention, there's nothing left to do but to tell him how you feel. This part will be hard, but you'll have to swallow your pride and get over the nervousness in your gut if you want results. Opening up and letting him know that you want to try again won't be easy, but it will be worth it. Here's how to do it:

Pick the right place and time. Try to get him alone at a time when he's in a good mood and when there isn't a chance his friends will be lurking in the background.

Swallow your pride. If you've made any mistakes, apologize for the past, and be as specific as possible to show that you're self-aware.

Be honest. Tell him that you really miss having him in your life, and that you made a big mistake and want him back.

Say that you want to make it up to him and to show him how much you've changed.

Keep him this time. If your former guy is receptive, then you'll start spending more time with him, whether he asks you out on a date or just spends more time with you in the company of others. You have to make the most of the time you have with him to make sure that you don't lose him again. Here's what you should do:

Don't repeat your mistakes. Remind yourself of what went wrong and vow not to do the same thing this time. Remember how hard you've tried to improve yourself.

Don't put too much pressure on yourself. If you're constantly worried about not messing up again, you won't be able to focus on the present.

Start fresh. Think of this as starting a brand-new relationship while having a bank of information to work with. Don't dwell on the past or rehash old arguments.

Be yourself. Though you're an improved version of yourself, you're still you at the end of the day, so remember to be the girl he fell for in the beginning. If you try too hard to prove how different you've become, you'll lose sight of who you are.

Know when to walk away. If you've tried everything and then some, but your former man still won't give you the time of day, then too much damage has been done for you to pursue the relationship further. If he's ignoring you, resisting your advances, or just downright being mean to you, then it's time to walk away before you get even more hurt.

Remember that not very relationship can be salvaged. You've done your best and can applaud yourself for trying.

Walk away with your head high. Don't be embarrassed about opening up and sharing your true feeling.

The End

Printed in Great Britain
by Amazon